I0480011

If you talk about it, it's a dream, if you envision it, it's

possible, but if you schedule it, it's real.

Tony Robbins

Hi, my names Hanna! Right now you're holding my
Reach Goals Faster planner in your hands, and I am SO
glad. I hope this planner can be your shortcut to a life you
really love, with all your heart!

I am extremely passionate about being able to help other
entrepreneurs move forward with their business. I can
clearly see a connection between people like you, and a
better world. I know you have important things to share.
You have insights, knowledge and experience that we
want to know more about!

Do you know how amazing life can be? Have you realized
that? And did you know that YOU hold the wheel and can
steer in whatever direction you want?

If you look around in nature you'll see that everything is
constantly changing. We are not the same person today as
we were yesterday. That's the change we're going to take
hold of and knowingly steer it in the way we wish it to go.

If we don't grow, we shrink. Nothing can stand still, the
only thing that is constant is change. What do you want to
do with your life? Grow or shrink?

Harness that energy of change - and make it an advantage
for you. Use that energy of change and let it be about
improvement.

As an entrepreneur you face the opportunity to really
succeed with your business and thus, pave a way for so, so
many others.

It was after a time in exhaustion/adrenal fatigue that I realized I needed to structure my life, and above all live and work in a way that didn't take energy from me, but GAVE it. Smarter, not harder.

I had a previous setback when well-meaning coaches and friends suggested that I should learn to plan my time better and be so boringly realistic. I'm a freedom lover of the highest rank, so I was not interested in all this about planning. HOWEVER. I am more interested in leaning how to work smarter, and not harder, than I am of refusing to change or to be right - so I tried planning. Thus, for the first time I discovered real freedom. I had more time for everything. I had better luck with pretty much everything I did, compared to before I learned how to plan smart.

I wanted more.
What you are now holding in your hand is my own combination of many different time management ideas among other things. Stephen Covey, the 12 week year and many other courses I went to and coaches I have had over the years. I work a lot on planning with my own clients, so the need for a planner that looks exactly like this was there to facilitate the process.

I myself continue to use the creative forces and the constant changes to
to grow as a human being and create a life that becomes richer and richer with each passing day.

If I can, so can you.

XO Hanna Horner

Daydream Book

Very little is needed to make a happy life;

it is all within yourself,

in your way of thinking.

Marcus Aurelius

Do you know who Grant Cardone is? He is one of North America's most successful real estate investors and he is the best in sales and sales training. Every morning he sits down and writes down his craziest goals and wildest daydreams. In one of his books he writes that this is just a habit, this "easy-to-skip-because-it "seems-totally-unnecessary-habit" that has led him to become so successful.

I have tried myself, and I have also gotten many of my clients up and running to begin writing a daydream book. The effect is incredibly large. So large that to have this dream and to feel like you're living in that dream-world is what I'm creating this planner to talk about.

That is why there is room for your daydreams in each day planner. Take a few minutes each morning and daydream. Leave that dream so vibrant that it feels like it is real, and you will see big changes in your life.

Objectives and Focus

If you don't know where you are going, you might wind up someplace else.

Yogi Berra

When we give ourselves something positive to focus on
for a day,
we can be mindful about putting one foot in front of the
other and making sure we are getting close to the result we
want.
When we know what we want, we are more likely to
succeed.

In addition, we save an incredible amount of time not
having to think about what to do "now".
It is already determined. You can simply do without any
hesitation or doubt. By the
way, the kick ass coach Mel Robbins teaches that we have
3 seconds to take action,
before we subconsciously start giving ourselves a
thousand reasons why it's a bad idea.
Therefore, it is even more important that we have a plan,
and take action just as it says in our plan - within three
seconds. Action cures fear very effectively.

Sometimes your goal for the day can be: "make the bed,
shower" - and sometimes it can be:
"Make peace on earth" it is entirely up to you. You do
your best every day,
that's good enough.

A great habit to adopt in to your morning routine is to
decide what your focus should be and what your goal of
the day is. Have a main focus, something you
absolutely must do to feel satisfied with the day.
Everything else is a bonus.

Of course, the focus of the day and everything you spend time on during the day should be fully in line with your goals (which you will be able to identify soon).

It is also important that we do not give ourselves too much time to complete a task. I mean that it's smart to make sure every minute of your day has a purpose. This way we make it harder for ourselves to deceive ourselves into thinking we can scroll facebook, fix a sixth cup of coffee, talk a little with mom or whatever it may be. If we want to do such things in a day (and sometimes you want to) you simply just have to schedule it. It sounds clumsy and deprivation in the beginning, but I promise it will make you more effective and give you even more freedom than you've ever had before.

It is also a good idea when you are still in the planning stage, that you are thinking about what to do and what order you want to do it in. Make sure you do not plan for too many things in a row that you know are draining you of energy. Put in something that gives you energy and something that feels neutral. Simply balance your day. Bonus if you can end each workday with something that gives you energy!

Evening Routine and Review

There's only one corner of the universe

you can be certain of improving, and that's your own self."

Aldous Huxley

Grant Cardone writes down his dreams even in the evening, I usually settle for writing down my WINS, ie things that I have done that have gotten really good results. Additionally
I reflect a little on what didn't go so well, and on how I can do it in a different, better way next time.

Before I fall asleep, I have also filled the body with a sense of gratitude. For example, I can feel gratitude for my family, something fun that happened, a beautiful sunset or a nice memory. It does not matter what arouses the feeling of gratitude in me, but it is the feeling itself that is important. This is about having the right mindset, and is essential for an entrepreneur who wants to achieve success and happiness.

80% of success consists of having the right mindset.

New Habits

We are not born with the habits we have. Our habits have nothing to do with our identity. Not even our thoughts that we think out of old habit, are who we really are.

We are free to pick and choose from our habits. We can choose habits that are self-destructive, or we can purposefully grind out the habits that create success and happiness in life something we do even without thinking about it. Like you're used to throwing yourself on the couch in a certain way, or how you dress in the morning (Which leg do you put down in your pants first? I bet it's always the same leg.)

Identify habits that you think could help you and your success. Do you want a stronger and healthier body? If so, just upgrade your habits around just that. Want to get more organized? Become a morning person? Yes, you name it.
You can do it.
It's just a habit.

This planner has a has a habit tracker for each week with room for three new habits. You decide on the habit you want to cultivate, and for each day you implement the new habit, you give yourself a checkmark.

12 Weeks

88% of all New Year's promises are broken. A year is simply not a realistic goal.

I caught myself planning for 12-week intervals after reading the book "the 12 week year". The layout for planning in the book itself was a bit stressed, masculine and wasn't a good fit for me at all - but the 12-week format felt completely

RIGHT.

You can use your 12 weeks in an incredibly effective way, you can see clear results and it is an appropriate time intervall in order to set new goals for each new 12-week interval. Besides, you get a little vacation here and there if you still want to stick to a calendar year. In other words, freedom and efficiency.

Imagine the feeling of having a New Year's Eve every 12 weeks! New promises, new energy and new sprint at the end.
How far do you want to get in 12 weeks? To answer that question you will want to keep track of what you dream of doing. What do you dream of having accomplished in 5 years?

If we imagine you actually managed to make your dream a reality, how far have you come in 4 years? 3 years? Start getting a little more realistic now, so here 3 years into the future, figure out how much money you need to make to live your dream life. Have you hired a team? Do you work solo? Have you expanded?

If you have come so far in 3 years, where will you be you in 2 years? In 12 months? How about 6?

How far will you have had to go in the next 12 weeks if this is exactly where you are in 6 months? I will guide you through this in this planner.

Frogs

If you have to choose between two frogs eat them both, and the ugliest one first.

Brian Tracy

Being an entrepreneur sometimes means that we have to do things that we really don't want to do and would rather postpone for the future. Sometimes this is because it is things that are outside our comfort zone, sometimes it is because we think it is boring as hell to deal with.

Those things are your frogs. It's the things we eat at least once every day. Frogs are energy thieves who give us a bad conscience and we save so much energy just dealing with them (eat the ones Brian Tracy writes about in his book Eat That Frog). Make it a habit to chew a frog every day, preferably at breakfast, and you will be surprised at how easy and fun everything else feels compared to it.

It's the habit of just dealing with things instead of procrastinating inevitable tasks, that get programmed when you learn this behaviour of eating frogs - and it's a good idea for anyone who wants to reach their goals - faster.

I am especially fond of the scary frogs. The things you are too uncertain or nervous to do. I can guarantee you that everything you want is outside your current comfort zone. Thus, you must be prepared to feel uncomfortable in order to to reach your goals. The sooner, the better. Chase fears and learn to act as if you already dared. It gives quick results, that's one thing that is absolutely certain.

12 Week To-Do Brain-Dump

The first step (after identifying where you want to be in 5 years, and identifying where you need to be in 12 weeks to make that possible) is to make a list of everything you imagine you need to do for to be able to row your projects ashore.
Unfiltered and all over the place works just fine. From this all over the place list, select:

Do Delay Delegate Delete

Do: Everything that only you (and only you) can do that needs to be done right now - which is profitable or important (ends on daily or weekly planning)

Delay: anything that only you (and only you) can do that can be scheduled - which is profitable or important (planned and scheduled but not in the next week or so)

Delegate: anything that anyone else can do better or as good as you and that must be done but which (preferably) is not very urgent - but still profitable or important.

Delete: everything else. Yes. Everything else. Maybe I can agree that it ends up in a list of future opportunities that you can develop if you run out of ideas.

Do the above exercise in a separate notepad and then enter the to-dos that survived here in your planner.

If you want, you can repeat Do, Delay, Delegate, Delete with all the things that you plan to do every week. Make sure that absolutely nothing gets thrown in to the planner without you checking it to be sure that it actually belongs. It is important that you spend your time solely on what you actually need to do.

Run with it now, and if you have any questions please email me hello@hannahorner.com

5 YEAR GOAL: _____

_____

WHY IS IT IMPORTANT FOR YOU TO SUCCEED
WITH THIS:
MILESTONES: _____

YEAR 4: _____

YEAR 3: _____

YEAR 2: _____

IN 4x12 WEEKS: _____

IN 3x12 WEEKS: _____

IN 2x12 WEEKS: _____

IN 12 WEEKS: _____

12 WEEK GOAL: _____

_____

WEEK 1 MILESTONE:
1:

2:

3:

WEEK 2 MILESTONE:

1:

2:

3:

WEEK 3 MILESTONE:

1:

2:

3:

WEEK 4 MILESTONE:

1:

2:

3:

WEEK 5 MILESTONE:
1:

2:

3:

WEEK 6 MILESTONE:

1:

2:

3:

WEEK 7 MILESTONE:

1:

2:

3:

WEEK 8 MILESTONE:

1:

2:

3:

WEEK 9 MILESTONE:
1:

2:

3:

WEEK 10 MILESTONE:

1:

2:

3:

WEEK 11 MILESTONE:

1:

2:

3:

WEEK 12 MILESTONE:

1:

2:

3:

WEEK 1
NEW HABITS/HABIT TRACKER MON - SUN

1 _____

2 _____

3 _____

WEEKLY INSIGHTS REVIEW:

MY 3 BIGGEST WINS:

1 _____

2 _____

3 _____

HOW SATISFIED AM I WITH MY EFFORTS? DID I
REALLY DO MY BEST? (ON A SCALE FROM 1-10 ,10
IS HUGE SATISFACTION)_____

HOW CAN I PLAN OUT MY NEXT WEEK TO MAKE
IT BETTER? _____

_____

WEEK 2
NEW HABITS/HABIT TRACKER MON - SUN

1 _____
2 _____
3 _____

WEEKLY INSIGHTS REVIEW:

MY 3 BIGGEST WINS:

1 _____

2 _____

3 _____

HOW SATISFIED AM I WITH MY EFFORTS? DID I
REALLY DO MY BEST? (ON A SCALE FROM 1-10 ,10
IS HUGE SATISFACTION)_____

HOW CAN I PLAN OUT MY NEXT WEEK TO MAKE
IT BETTER? _____

_____

WEEK 3
NEW HABITS/HABIT TRACKER MON - SUN

1 _____

2 _____

3 _____

WEEKLY INSIGHTS REVIEW:

MY 3 BIGGEST WINS:

1 _____

2 _____

3 _____

HOW SATISFIED AM I WITH MY EFFORTS? DID I
REALLY DO MY BEST? (ON A SCALE FROM 1-10 ,10
IS HUGE SATISFACTION)_____

HOW CAN I PLAN OUT MY NEXT WEEK TO MAKE
IT BETTER? _____

_____

WEEK 4
NEW HABITS/HABIT TRACKER MON - SUN

1 _____

2 _____

3 _____

WEEKLY INSIGHTS REVIEW:

MY 3 BIGGEST WINS:

1 _____

2 _____

3 _____

HOW SATISFIED AM I WITH MY EFFORTS? DID I
REALLY DO MY BEST? (ON A SCALE FROM 1-10 ,10
IS HUGE SATISFACTION)_____

HOW CAN I PLAN OUT MY NEXT WEEK TO MAKE
IT BETTER? _____

WEEK 5
NEW HABITS/HABIT TRACKER MON - SUN

1 _____

2 _____

3 _____

WEEKLY INSIGHTS REVIEW:

MY 3 BIGGEST WINS:

1 _____

2 _____

3 _____

HOW SATISFIED AM I WITH MY EFFORTS? DID I
REALLY DO MY BEST? (ON A SCALE FROM 1-10 ,10
IS HUGE SATISFACTION)_____

HOW CAN I PLAN OUT MY NEXT WEEK TO MAKE
IT BETTER? _____

_____

WEEK 6
NEW HABITS/HABIT TRACKER MON - SUN

1 _____
2 _____
3 _____

WEEKLY INSIGHTS REVIEW:

MY 3 BIGGEST WINS:

1 _____

2 _____

3 _____

HOW SATISFIED AM I WITH MY EFFORTS? DID I
REALLY DO MY BEST? (ON A SCALE FROM 1-10 ,10
IS HUGE SATISFACTION)_____

HOW CAN I PLAN OUT MY NEXT WEEK TO MAKE
IT BETTER? _____

_____

WEEK 7
NEW HABITS/HABIT TRACKER MON - SUN

1 _____

2 _____

3 _____

WEEKLY INSIGHTS REVIEW:

MY 3 BIGGEST WINS:

1 _____

2 _____

3 _____

HOW SATISFIED AM I WITH MY EFFORTS? DID I
REALLY DO MY BEST? (ON A SCALE FROM 1-10 ,10
IS HUGE SATISFACTION)_____

HOW CAN I PLAN OUT MY NEXT WEEK TO MAKE
IT BETTER? _____

_____

WEEK 8
NEW HABITS/HABIT TRACKER MON - SUN

1 _____
2 _____
3 _____

WEEKLY INSIGHTS REVIEW:

MY 3 BIGGEST WINS:

1 _____

2 _____

3 _____

HOW SATISFIED AM I WITH MY EFFORTS? DID I
REALLY DO MY BEST? (ON A SCALE FROM 1-10 ,10
IS HUGE SATISFACTION)_____

HOW CAN I PLAN OUT MY NEXT WEEK TO MAKE
IT BETTER? _____

_____

WEEK 9
NEW HABITS/HABIT TRACKER MON - SUN

1 _____

2 _____

3 _____

WEEKLY INSIGHTS REVIEW:

MY 3 BIGGEST WINS:

1 _____

2 _____

3 _____

HOW SATISFIED AM I WITH MY EFFORTS? DID I
REALLY DO MY BEST? (ON A SCALE FROM 1-10 ,10
IS HUGE SATISFACTION)_____

HOW CAN I PLAN OUT MY NEXT WEEK TO MAKE
IT BETTER? _____

_____

WEEK 10
NEW HABITS/HABIT TRACKER MON - SUN

1 _____
2 _____
3 _____

WEEKLY INSIGHTS REVIEW:

MY 3 BIGGEST WINS:

1 _____

2 _____

3 _____

HOW SATISFIED AM I WITH MY EFFORTS? DID I
REALLY DO MY BEST? (ON A SCALE FROM 1-10 ,10
IS HUGE SATISFACTION)_____

HOW CAN I PLAN OUT MY NEXT WEEK TO MAKE
IT BETTER? _____

_____

WEEK 11
NEW HABITS/HABIT TRACKER MON - SUN

1 _____

2 _____

3 _____

WEEKLY INSIGHTS REVIEW:

MY 3 BIGGEST WINS:

1 _____

2 _____

3 _____

HOW SATISFIED AM I WITH MY EFFORTS? DID I
REALLY DO MY BEST? (ON A SCALE FROM 1-10 ,10
IS HUGE SATISFACTION)_____

HOW CAN I PLAN OUT MY NEXT WEEK TO MAKE
IT BETTER? _____

_____

WEEK 12
NEW HABITS/HABIT TRACKER MON - SUN

1 _____
2 _____
3 _____

WEEKLY INSIGHTS REVIEW:

MY 3 BIGGEST WINS:

1 _____

2 _____

3 _____

HOW SATISFIED AM I WITH MY EFFORTS? DID I
REALLY DO MY BEST? (ON A SCALE FROM 1-10 ,10
IS HUGE SATISFACTION)_____

HOW CAN I PLAN OUT MY NEXT WEEK TO MAKE
IT BETTER? _____

_____

DATE: WEEK:

TODAY I FEEL (ON A SCALE FROM 1- 10): TO
INCREASE MY ENERGY I CAN:

WILD DAYDREAMS:

TODAYS MAIN OBJECTIVE AND FOCUS:

FROG OF THE DAY:

OTHER TO-DOS & BRAIN DUMP (NOTES):

6.00-6.30	
6.30-7.00	
7.00-7.30	
7.30-8.00	
8.00-8.30	
8.30-9.00	
9.00-9.30	
9.30-10.00	
10.00-10.30	
10.30-11.00	
11.00-11.30	
11.30-12.00	
12.00-12.30	
12.30-13.00	
13.00-13.30	
13.30-14.00	
14.00-14.30	
14.30-15.00	
15.00-15.30	
15.30-16.00	
16.00-16.30	
16.30-17.00	
17.30-18.00	
18.00-18.30	
18.30-19.00	
19.00-19.30	
19.30-20.00	
20.00-20.30	
20.30-21.00	

DATE: WEEK:

TODAY I FEEL (ON A SCALE FROM 1- 10): TO
INCREASE MY ENERGY I CAN:

WILD DAYDREAMS:

TODAYS MAIN OBJECTIVE AND FOCUS:

FROG OF THE DAY:

OTHER TO-DOS & BRAIN DUMP (NOTES):

6.00-6.30	
6.30-7.00	
7.00-7.30	
7.30-8.00	
8.00-8.30	
8.30-9.00	
9.00-9.30	
9.30-10.00	
10.00-10.30	
10.30-11.00	
11.00-11.30	
11.30-12.00	
12.00-12.30	
12.30-13.00	
13.00-13.30	
13.30-14.00	
14.00-14.30	
14.30-15.00	
15.00-15.30	
15.30-16.00	
16.00-16.30	
16.30-17.00	
17.30-18.00	
18.00-18.30	
18.30-19.00	
19.00-19.30	
19.30-20.00	
20.00-20.30	
20.30-21.00	

DATE: WEEK:

TODAY I FEEL (ON A SCALE FROM 1- 10): TO
INCREASE MY ENERGY I CAN:

WILD DAYDREAMS:

TODAYS MAIN OBJECTIVE AND FOCUS:

FROG OF THE DAY:

OTHER TO-DOS & BRAIN DUMP (NOTES):

6.00-6.30	
6.30-7.00	
7.00-7.30	
7.30-8.00	
8.00-8.30	
8.30-9.00	
9.00-9.30	
9.30-10.00	
10.00-10.30	
10.30-11.00	
11.00-11.30	
11.30-12.00	
12.00-12.30	
12.30-13.00	
13.00-13.30	
13.30-14.00	
14.00-14.30	
14.30-15.00	
15.00-15.30	
15.30-16.00	
16.00-16.30	
16.30-17.00	
17.30-18.00	
18.00-18.30	
18.30-19.00	
19.00-19.30	
19.30-20.00	
20.00-20.30	
20.30-21.00	

DATE: WEEK:

TODAY I FEEL (ON A SCALE FROM 1- 10): TO
INCREASE MY ENERGY I CAN:

WILD DAYDREAMS:

TODAYS MAIN OBJECTIVE AND FOCUS:

FROG OF THE DAY:

OTHER TO-DOS & BRAIN DUMP (NOTES):

Time	
6.00-6.30	
6.30-7.00	
7.00-7.30	
7.30-8.00	
8.00-8.30	
8.30-9.00	
9.00-9.30	
9.30-10.00	
10.00-10.30	
10.30-11.00	
11.00-11.30	
11.30-12.00	
12.00-12.30	
12.30-13.00	
13.00-13.30	
13.30-14.00	
14.00-14.30	
14.30-15.00	
15.00-15.30	
15.30-16.00	
16.00-16.30	
16.30-17.00	
17.30-18.00	
18.00-18.30	
18.30-19.00	
19.00-19.30	
19.30-20.00	
20.00-20.30	
20.30-21.00	

DATE: WEEK:

TODAY I FEEL (ON A SCALE FROM 1- 10): TO
INCREASE MY ENERGY I CAN:

WILD DAYDREAMS:

TODAYS MAIN OBJECTIVE AND FOCUS:

FROG OF THE DAY:

OTHER TO-DOS & BRAIN DUMP (NOTES):

6.00-6.30	
6.30-7.00	
7.00-7.30	
7.30-8.00	
8.00-8.30	
8.30-9.00	
9.00-9.30	
9.30-10.00	
10.00-10.30	
10.30-11.00	
11.00-11.30	
11.30-12.00	
12.00-12.30	
12.30-13.00	
13.00-13.30	
13.30-14.00	
14.00-14.30	
14.30-15.00	
15.00-15.30	
15.30-16.00	
16.00-16.30	
16.30-17.00	
17.30-18.00	
18.00-18.30	
18.30-19.00	
19.00-19.30	
19.30-20.00	
20.00-20.30	
20.30-21.00	

DATE: WEEK:

TODAY I FEEL (ON A SCALE FROM 1- 10): TO
INCREASE MY ENERGY I CAN:

WILD DAYDREAMS:

TODAYS MAIN OBJECTIVE AND FOCUS:

FROG OF THE DAY:

OTHER TO-DOS & BRAIN DUMP (NOTES):

6.00-6.30	
6.30-7.00	
7.00-7.30	
7.30-8.00	
8.00-8.30	
8.30-9.00	
9.00-9.30	
9.30-10.00	
10.00-10.30	
10.30-11.00	
11.00-11.30	
11.30-12.00	
12.00-12.30	
12.30-13.00	
13.00-13.30	
13.30-14.00	
14.00-14.30	
14.30-15.00	
15.00-15.30	
15.30-16.00	
16.00-16.30	
16.30-17.00	
17.30-18.00	
18.00-18.30	
18.30-19.00	
19.00-19.30	
19.30-20.00	
20.00-20.30	
20.30-21.00	

DATE: WEEK:

TODAY I FEEL (ON A SCALE FROM 1- 10): TO
INCREASE MY ENERGY I CAN:

WILD DAYDREAMS:

TODAYS MAIN OBJECTIVE AND FOCUS:

FROG OF THE DAY:

OTHER TO-DOS & BRAIN DUMP (NOTES):

6.00-6.30	
6.30-7.00	
7.00-7.30	
7.30-8.00	
8.00-8.30	
8.30-9.00	
9.00-9.30	
9.30-10.00	
10.00-10.30	
10.30-11.00	
11.00-11.30	
11.30-12.00	
12.00-12.30	
12.30-13.00	
13.00-13.30	
13.30-14.00	
14.00-14.30	
14.30-15.00	
15.00-15.30	
15.30-16.00	
16.00-16.30	
16.30-17.00	
17.30-18.00	
18.00-18.30	
18.30-19.00	
19.00-19.30	
19.30-20.00	
20.00-20.30	
20.30-21.00	

DATE: WEEK:

TODAY I FEEL (ON A SCALE FROM 1- 10): TO
INCREASE MY ENERGY I CAN:

WILD DAYDREAMS:

TODAYS MAIN OBJECTIVE AND FOCUS:

FROG OF THE DAY:

OTHER TO-DOS & BRAIN DUMP (NOTES):

6.00-6.30	
6.30-7.00	
7.00-7.30	
7.30-8.00	
8.00-8.30	
8.30-9.00	
9.00-9.30	
9.30-10.00	
10.00-10.30	
10.30-11.00	
11.00-11.30	
11.30-12.00	
12.00-12.30	
12.30-13.00	
13.00-13.30	
13.30-14.00	
14.00-14.30	
14.30-15.00	
15.00-15.30	
15.30-16.00	
16.00-16.30	
16.30-17.00	
17.30-18.00	
18.00-18.30	
18.30-19.00	
19.00-19.30	
19.30-20.00	
20.00-20.30	
20.30-21.00	

DATE: WEEK:

TODAY I FEEL (ON A SCALE FROM 1- 10): TO
INCREASE MY ENERGY I CAN:

WILD DAYDREAMS:

TODAYS MAIN OBJECTIVE AND FOCUS:

FROG OF THE DAY:

OTHER TO-DOS & BRAIN DUMP (NOTES):

Time	
6.00-6.30	
6.30-7.00	
7.00-7.30	
7.30-8.00	
8.00-8.30	
8.30-9.00	
9.00-9.30	
9.30-10.00	
10.00-10.30	
10.30-11.00	
11.00-11.30	
11.30-12.00	
12.00-12.30	
12.30-13.00	
13.00-13.30	
13.30-14.00	
14.00-14.30	
14.30-15.00	
15.00-15.30	
15.30-16.00	
16.00-16.30	
16.30-17.00	
17.30-18.00	
18.00-18.30	
18.30-19.00	
19.00-19.30	
19.30-20.00	
20.00-20.30	
20.30-21.00	

DATE: WEEK:

TODAY I FEEL (ON A SCALE FROM 1- 10): TO
INCREASE MY ENERGY I CAN:

WILD DAYDREAMS:

TODAYS MAIN OBJECTIVE AND FOCUS:

FROG OF THE DAY:

OTHER TO-DOS & BRAIN DUMP (NOTES):

6.00-6.30	
6.30-7.00	
7.00-7.30	
7.30-8.00	
8.00-8.30	
8.30-9.00	
9.00-9.30	
9.30-10.00	
10.00-10.30	
10.30-11.00	
11.00-11.30	
11.30-12.00	
12.00-12.30	
12.30-13.00	
13.00-13.30	
13.30-14.00	
14.00-14.30	
14.30-15.00	
15.00-15.30	
15.30-16.00	
16.00-16.30	
16.30-17.00	
17.30-18.00	
18.00-18.30	
18.30-19.00	
19.00-19.30	
19.30-20.00	
20.00-20.30	
20.30-21.00	

DATE: WEEK:

TODAY I FEEL (ON A SCALE FROM 1- 10): TO
INCREASE MY ENERGY I CAN:

WILD DAYDREAMS:

TODAYS MAIN OBJECTIVE AND FOCUS:

FROG OF THE DAY:

OTHER TO-DOS & BRAIN DUMP (NOTES):

6.00-6.30	
6.30-7.00	
7.00-7.30	
7.30-8.00	
8.00-8.30	
8.30-9.00	
9.00-9.30	
9.30-10.00	
10.00-10.30	
10.30-11.00	
11.00-11.30	
11.30-12.00	
12.00-12.30	
12.30-13.00	
13.00-13.30	
13.30-14.00	
14.00-14.30	
14.30-15.00	
15.00-15.30	
15.30-16.00	
16.00-16.30	
16.30-17.00	
17.30-18.00	
18.00-18.30	
18.30-19.00	
19.00-19.30	
19.30-20.00	
20.00-20.30	
20.30-21.00	

DATE: WEEK:

TODAY I FEEL (ON A SCALE FROM 1- 10): TO
INCREASE MY ENERGY I CAN:

WILD DAYDREAMS:

TODAYS MAIN OBJECTIVE AND FOCUS:

FROG OF THE DAY:

OTHER TO-DOS & BRAIN DUMP (NOTES):

Time	
6.00-6.30	
6.30-7.00	
7.00-7.30	
7.30-8.00	
8.00-8.30	
8.30-9.00	
9.00-9.30	
9.30-10.00	
10.00-10.30	
10.30-11.00	
11.00-11.30	
11.30-12.00	
12.00-12.30	
12.30-13.00	
13.00-13.30	
13.30-14.00	
14.00-14.30	
14.30-15.00	
15.00-15.30	
15.30-16.00	
16.00-16.30	
16.30-17.00	
17.30-18.00	
18.00-18.30	
18.30-19.00	
19.00-19.30	
19.30-20.00	
20.00-20.30	
20.30-21.00	

DATE: WEEK:

TODAY I FEEL (ON A SCALE FROM 1- 10): TO
INCREASE MY ENERGY I CAN:

WILD DAYDREAMS:

TODAYS MAIN OBJECTIVE AND FOCUS:

FROG OF THE DAY:

OTHER TO-DOS & BRAIN DUMP (NOTES):

6.00-6.30	
6.30-7.00	
7.00-7.30	
7.30-8.00	
8.00-8.30	
8.30-9.00	
9.00-9.30	
9.30-10.00	
10.00-10.30	
10.30-11.00	
11.00-11.30	
11.30-12.00	
12.00-12.30	
12.30-13.00	
13.00-13.30	
13.30-14.00	
14.00-14.30	
14.30-15.00	
15.00-15.30	
15.30-16.00	
16.00-16.30	
16.30-17.00	
17.30-18.00	
18.00-18.30	
18.30-19.00	
19.00-19.30	
19.30-20.00	
20.00-20.30	
20.30-21.00	

DATE: WEEK:

TODAY I FEEL (ON A SCALE FROM 1- 10): TO
INCREASE MY ENERGY I CAN:

WILD DAYDREAMS:

TODAYS MAIN OBJECTIVE AND FOCUS:

FROG OF THE DAY:

OTHER TO-DOS & BRAIN DUMP (NOTES):

6.00-6.30	
6.30-7.00	
7.00-7.30	
7.30-8.00	
8.00-8.30	
8.30-9.00	
9.00-9.30	
9.30-10.00	
10.00-10.30	
10.30-11.00	
11.00-11.30	
11.30-12.00	
12.00-12.30	
12.30-13.00	
13.00-13.30	
13.30-14.00	
14.00-14.30	
14.30-15.00	
15.00-15.30	
15.30-16.00	
16.00-16.30	
16.30-17.00	
17.30-18.00	
18.00-18.30	
18.30-19.00	
19.00-19.30	
19.30-20.00	
20.00-20.30	
20.30-21.00	

DATE: WEEK:

TODAY I FEEL (ON A SCALE FROM 1- 10): TO
INCREASE MY ENERGY I CAN:

WILD DAYDREAMS:

TODAYS MAIN OBJECTIVE AND FOCUS:

FROG OF THE DAY:

OTHER TO-DOS & BRAIN DUMP (NOTES):

6.00-6.30	
6.30-7.00	
7.00-7.30	
7.30-8.00	
8.00-8.30	
8.30-9.00	
9.00-9.30	
9.30-10.00	
10.00-10.30	
10.30-11.00	
11.00-11.30	
11.30-12.00	
12.00-12.30	
12.30-13.00	
13.00-13.30	
13.30-14.00	
14.00-14.30	
14.30-15.00	
15.00-15.30	
15.30-16.00	
16.00-16.30	
16.30-17.00	
17.30-18.00	
18.00-18.30	
18.30-19.00	
19.00-19.30	
19.30-20.00	
20.00-20.30	
20.30-21.00	

DATE: WEEK:

TODAY I FEEL (ON A SCALE FROM 1- 10): TO
INCREASE MY ENERGY I CAN:

WILD DAYDREAMS:

TODAYS MAIN OBJECTIVE AND FOCUS:

FROG OF THE DAY:

OTHER TO-DOS & BRAIN DUMP (NOTES):

6.00-6.30	
6.30-7.00	
7.00-7.30	
7.30-8.00	
8.00-8.30	
8.30-9.00	
9.00-9.30	
9.30-10.00	
10.00-10.30	
10.30-11.00	
11.00-11.30	
11.30-12.00	
12.00-12.30	
12.30-13.00	
13.00-13.30	
13.30-14.00	
14.00-14.30	
14.30-15.00	
15.00-15.30	
15.30-16.00	
16.00-16.30	
16.30-17.00	
17.30-18.00	
18.00-18.30	
18.30-19.00	
19.00-19.30	
19.30-20.00	
20.00-20.30	
20.30-21.00	

DATE: WEEK:

TODAY I FEEL (ON A SCALE FROM 1- 10): TO
INCREASE MY ENERGY I CAN:

WILD DAYDREAMS:

TODAYS MAIN OBJECTIVE AND FOCUS:

FROG OF THE DAY:

OTHER TO-DOS & BRAIN DUMP (NOTES):

6.00-6.30	
6.30-7.00	
7.00-7.30	
7.30-8.00	
8.00-8.30	
8.30-9.00	
9.00-9.30	
9.30-10.00	
10.00-10.30	
10.30-11.00	
11.00-11.30	
11.30-12.00	
12.00-12.30	
12.30-13.00	
13.00-13.30	
13.30-14.00	
14.00-14.30	
14.30-15.00	
15.00-15.30	
15.30-16.00	
16.00-16.30	
16.30-17.00	
17.30-18.00	
18.00-18.30	
18.30-19.00	
19.00-19.30	
19.30-20.00	
20.00-20.30	
20.30-21.00	

DATE: WEEK:

TODAY I FEEL (ON A SCALE FROM 1- 10): TO
INCREASE MY ENERGY I CAN:

WILD DAYDREAMS:

TODAYS MAIN OBJECTIVE AND FOCUS:

FROG OF THE DAY:

OTHER TO-DOS & BRAIN DUMP (NOTES):

6.00-6.30	
6.30-7.00	
7.00-7.30	
7.30-8.00	
8.00-8.30	
8.30-9.00	
9.00-9.30	
9.30-10.00	
10.00-10.30	
10.30-11.00	
11.00-11.30	
11.30-12.00	
12.00-12.30	
12.30-13.00	
13.00-13.30	
13.30-14.00	
14.00-14.30	
14.30-15.00	
15.00-15.30	
15.30-16.00	
16.00-16.30	
16.30-17.00	
17.30-18.00	
18.00-18.30	
18.30-19.00	
19.00-19.30	
19.30-20.00	
20.00-20.30	
20.30-21.00	

DATE: WEEK:

TODAY I FEEL (ON A SCALE FROM 1- 10): TO
INCREASE MY ENERGY I CAN:

WILD DAYDREAMS:

TODAYS MAIN OBJECTIVE AND FOCUS:

FROG OF THE DAY:

OTHER TO-DOS & BRAIN DUMP (NOTES):

6.00-6.30	
6.30-7.00	
7.00-7.30	
7.30-8.00	
8.00-8.30	
8.30-9.00	
9.00-9.30	
9.30-10.00	
10.00-10.30	
10.30-11.00	
11.00-11.30	
11.30-12.00	
12.00-12.30	
12.30-13.00	
13.00-13.30	
13.30-14.00	
14.00-14.30	
14.30-15.00	
15.00-15.30	
15.30-16.00	
16.00-16.30	
16.30-17.00	
17.30-18.00	
18.00-18.30	
18.30-19.00	
19.00-19.30	
19.30-20.00	
20.00-20.30	
20.30-21.00	

DATE: WEEK:

TODAY I FEEL (ON A SCALE FROM 1- 10): TO
INCREASE MY ENERGY I CAN:

WILD DAYDREAMS:

TODAYS MAIN OBJECTIVE AND FOCUS:

FROG OF THE DAY:

OTHER TO-DOS & BRAIN DUMP (NOTES):

6.00-6.30	
6.30-7.00	
7.00-7.30	
7.30-8.00	
8.00-8.30	
8.30-9.00	
9.00-9.30	
9.30-10.00	
10.00-10.30	
10.30-11.00	
11.00-11.30	
11.30-12.00	
12.00-12.30	
12.30-13.00	
13.00-13.30	
13.30-14.00	
14.00-14.30	
14.30-15.00	
15.00-15.30	
15.30-16.00	
16.00-16.30	
16.30-17.00	
17.30-18.00	
18.00-18.30	
18.30-19.00	
19.00-19.30	
19.30-20.00	
20.00-20.30	
20.30-21.00	

DATE: WEEK:

TODAY I FEEL (ON A SCALE FROM 1- 10): TO
INCREASE MY ENERGY I CAN:

WILD DAYDREAMS:

TODAYS MAIN OBJECTIVE AND FOCUS:

FROG OF THE DAY:

OTHER TO-DOS & BRAIN DUMP (NOTES):

6.00-6.30	
6.30-7.00	
7.00-7.30	
7.30-8.00	
8.00-8.30	
8.30-9.00	
9.00-9.30	
9.30-10.00	
10.00-10.30	
10.30-11.00	
11.00-11.30	
11.30-12.00	
12.00-12.30	
12.30-13.00	
13.00-13.30	
13.30-14.00	
14.00-14.30	
14.30-15.00	
15.00-15.30	
15.30-16.00	
16.00-16.30	
16.30-17.00	
17.30-18.00	
18.00-18.30	
18.30-19.00	
19.00-19.30	
19.30-20.00	
20.00-20.30	
20.30-21.00	

DATE: WEEK:

TODAY I FEEL (ON A SCALE FROM 1- 10): TO
INCREASE MY ENERGY I CAN:

WILD DAYDREAMS:

TODAYS MAIN OBJECTIVE AND FOCUS:

FROG OF THE DAY:

OTHER TO-DOS & BRAIN DUMP (NOTES):

6.00-6.30	
6.30-7.00	
7.00-7.30	
7.30-8.00	
8.00-8.30	
8.30-9.00	
9.00-9.30	
9.30-10.00	
10.00-10.30	
10.30-11.00	
11.00-11.30	
11.30-12.00	
12.00-12.30	
12.30-13.00	
13.00-13.30	
13.30-14.00	
14.00-14.30	
14.30-15.00	
15.00-15.30	
15.30-16.00	
16.00-16.30	
16.30-17.00	
17.30-18.00	
18.00-18.30	
18.30-19.00	
19.00-19.30	
19.30-20.00	
20.00-20.30	
20.30-21.00	

DATE: WEEK:

TODAY I FEEL (ON A SCALE FROM 1- 10): TO
INCREASE MY ENERGY I CAN:

WILD DAYDREAMS:

TODAYS MAIN OBJECTIVE AND FOCUS:

FROG OF THE DAY:

OTHER TO-DOS & BRAIN DUMP (NOTES):

6.00-6.30	
6.30-7.00	
7.00-7.30	
7.30-8.00	
8.00-8.30	
8.30-9.00	
9.00-9.30	
9.30-10.00	
10.00-10.30	
10.30-11.00	
11.00-11.30	
11.30-12.00	
12.00-12.30	
12.30-13.00	
13.00-13.30	
13.30-14.00	
14.00-14.30	
14.30-15.00	
15.00-15.30	
15.30-16.00	
16.00-16.30	
16.30-17.00	
17.30-18.00	
18.00-18.30	
18.30-19.00	
19.00-19.30	
19.30-20.00	
20.00-20.30	
20.30-21.00	

DATE: WEEK:

TODAY I FEEL (ON A SCALE FROM 1- 10): TO
INCREASE MY ENERGY I CAN:

WILD DAYDREAMS:

TODAYS MAIN OBJECTIVE AND FOCUS:

FROG OF THE DAY:

OTHER TO-DOS & BRAIN DUMP (NOTES):

Time	
6.00-6.30	
6.30-7.00	
7.00-7.30	
7.30-8.00	
8.00-8.30	
8.30-9.00	
9.00-9.30	
9.30-10.00	
10.00-10.30	
10.30-11.00	
11.00-11.30	
11.30-12.00	
12.00-12.30	
12.30-13.00	
13.00-13.30	
13.30-14.00	
14.00-14.30	
14.30-15.00	
15.00-15.30	
15.30-16.00	
16.00-16.30	
16.30-17.00	
17.30-18.00	
18.00-18.30	
18.30-19.00	
19.00-19.30	
19.30-20.00	
20.00-20.30	
20.30-21.00	

DATE: WEEK:

TODAY I FEEL (ON A SCALE FROM 1- 10): TO
INCREASE MY ENERGY I CAN:

WILD DAYDREAMS:

TODAYS MAIN OBJECTIVE AND FOCUS:

FROG OF THE DAY:

OTHER TO-DOS & BRAIN DUMP (NOTES):

6.00-6.30	
6.30-7.00	
7.00-7.30	
7.30-8.00	
8.00-8.30	
8.30-9.00	
9.00-9.30	
9.30-10.00	
10.00-10.30	
10.30-11.00	
11.00-11.30	
11.30-12.00	
12.00-12.30	
12.30-13.00	
13.00-13.30	
13.30-14.00	
14.00-14.30	
14.30-15.00	
15.00-15.30	
15.30-16.00	
16.00-16.30	
16.30-17.00	
17.30-18.00	
18.00-18.30	
18.30-19.00	
19.00-19.30	
19.30-20.00	
20.00-20.30	
20.30-21.00	

DATE: WEEK:

TODAY I FEEL (ON A SCALE FROM 1- 10): TO
INCREASE MY ENERGY I CAN:

WILD DAYDREAMS:

TODAYS MAIN OBJECTIVE AND FOCUS:

FROG OF THE DAY:

OTHER TO-DOS & BRAIN DUMP (NOTES):

6.00-6.30	
6.30-7.00	
7.00-7.30	
7.30-8.00	
8.00-8.30	
8.30-9.00	
9.00-9.30	
9.30-10.00	
10.00-10.30	
10.30-11.00	
11.00-11.30	
11.30-12.00	
12.00-12.30	
12.30-13.00	
13.00-13.30	
13.30-14.00	
14.00-14.30	
14.30-15.00	
15.00-15.30	
15.30-16.00	
16.00-16.30	
16.30-17.00	
17.30-18.00	
18.00-18.30	
18.30-19.00	
19.00-19.30	
19.30-20.00	
20.00-20.30	
20.30-21.00	

DATE: WEEK:

TODAY I FEEL (ON A SCALE FROM 1- 10): TO
INCREASE MY ENERGY I CAN:

WILD DAYDREAMS:

TODAYS MAIN OBJECTIVE AND FOCUS:

FROG OF THE DAY:

OTHER TO-DOS & BRAIN DUMP (NOTES):

6.00-6.30	
6.30-7.00	
7.00-7.30	
7.30-8.00	
8.00-8.30	
8.30-9.00	
9.00-9.30	
9.30-10.00	
10.00-10.30	
10.30-11.00	
11.00-11.30	
11.30-12.00	
12.00-12.30	
12.30-13.00	
13.00-13.30	
13.30-14.00	
14.00-14.30	
14.30-15.00	
15.00-15.30	
15.30-16.00	
16.00-16.30	
16.30-17.00	
17.30-18.00	
18.00-18.30	
18.30-19.00	
19.00-19.30	
19.30-20.00	
20.00-20.30	
20.30-21.00	

DATE: WEEK:

TODAY I FEEL (ON A SCALE FROM 1- 10): TO
INCREASE MY ENERGY I CAN:

WILD DAYDREAMS:

TODAYS MAIN OBJECTIVE AND FOCUS:

FROG OF THE DAY:

OTHER TO-DOS & BRAIN DUMP (NOTES):

6.00-6.30	
6.30-7.00	
7.00-7.30	
7.30-8.00	
8.00-8.30	
8.30-9.00	
9.00-9.30	
9.30-10.00	
10.00-10.30	
10.30-11.00	
11.00-11.30	
11.30-12.00	
12.00-12.30	
12.30-13.00	
13.00-13.30	
13.30-14.00	
14.00-14.30	
14.30-15.00	
15.00-15.30	
15.30-16.00	
16.00-16.30	
16.30-17.00	
17.30-18.00	
18.00-18.30	
18.30-19.00	
19.00-19.30	
19.30-20.00	
20.00-20.30	
20.30-21.00	

DATE: WEEK:

TODAY I FEEL (ON A SCALE FROM 1- 10): TO
INCREASE MY ENERGY I CAN:

WILD DAYDREAMS:

TODAYS MAIN OBJECTIVE AND FOCUS:

FROG OF THE DAY:

OTHER TO-DOS & BRAIN DUMP (NOTES):

Time	
6.00-6.30	
6.30-7.00	
7.00-7.30	
7.30-8.00	
8.00-8.30	
8.30-9.00	
9.00-9.30	
9.30-10.00	
10.00-10.30	
10.30-11.00	
11.00-11.30	
11.30-12.00	
12.00-12.30	
12.30-13.00	
13.00-13.30	
13.30-14.00	
14.00-14.30	
14.30-15.00	
15.00-15.30	
15.30-16.00	
16.00-16.30	
16.30-17.00	
17.30-18.00	
18.00-18.30	
18.30-19.00	
19.00-19.30	
19.30-20.00	
20.00-20.30	
20.30-21.00	

DATE: WEEK:

TODAY I FEEL (ON A SCALE FROM 1- 10): TO
INCREASE MY ENERGY I CAN:

WILD DAYDREAMS:

TODAYS MAIN OBJECTIVE AND FOCUS:

FROG OF THE DAY:

OTHER TO-DOS & BRAIN DUMP (NOTES):

6.00-6.30	
6.30-7.00	
7.00-7.30	
7.30-8.00	
8.00-8.30	
8.30-9.00	
9.00-9.30	
9.30-10.00	
10.00-10.30	
10.30-11.00	
11.00-11.30	
11.30-12.00	
12.00-12.30	
12.30-13.00	
13.00-13.30	
13.30-14.00	
14.00-14.30	
14.30-15.00	
15.00-15.30	
15.30-16.00	
16.00-16.30	
16.30-17.00	
17.30-18.00	
18.00-18.30	
18.30-19.00	
19.00-19.30	
19.30-20.00	
20.00-20.30	
20.30-21.00	

DATE: WEEK:

TODAY I FEEL (ON A SCALE FROM 1- 10): TO
INCREASE MY ENERGY I CAN:

WILD DAYDREAMS:

TODAYS MAIN OBJECTIVE AND FOCUS:

FROG OF THE DAY:

OTHER TO-DOS & BRAIN DUMP (NOTES):

6.00-6.30	
6.30-7.00	
7.00-7.30	
7.30-8.00	
8.00-8.30	
8.30-9.00	
9.00-9.30	
9.30-10.00	
10.00-10.30	
10.30-11.00	
11.00-11.30	
11.30-12.00	
12.00-12.30	
12.30-13.00	
13.00-13.30	
13.30-14.00	
14.00-14.30	
14.30-15.00	
15.00-15.30	
15.30-16.00	
16.00-16.30	
16.30-17.00	
17.30-18.00	
18.00-18.30	
18.30-19.00	
19.00-19.30	
19.30-20.00	
20.00-20.30	
20.30-21.00	

DATE: WEEK:

TODAY I FEEL (ON A SCALE FROM 1- 10): TO
INCREASE MY ENERGY I CAN:

WILD DAYDREAMS:

TODAYS MAIN OBJECTIVE AND FOCUS:

FROG OF THE DAY:

OTHER TO-DOS & BRAIN DUMP (NOTES):

6.00-6.30	
6.30-7.00	
7.00-7.30	
7.30-8.00	
8.00-8.30	
8.30-9.00	
9.00-9.30	
9.30-10.00	
10.00-10.30	
10.30-11.00	
11.00-11.30	
11.30-12.00	
12.00-12.30	
12.30-13.00	
13.00-13.30	
13.30-14.00	
14.00-14.30	
14.30-15.00	
15.00-15.30	
15.30-16.00	
16.00-16.30	
16.30-17.00	
17.30-18.00	
18.00-18.30	
18.30-19.00	
19.00-19.30	
19.30-20.00	
20.00-20.30	
20.30-21.00	

DATE: WEEK:

TODAY I FEEL (ON A SCALE FROM 1- 10): TO
INCREASE MY ENERGY I CAN:

WILD DAYDREAMS:

TODAYS MAIN OBJECTIVE AND FOCUS:

FROG OF THE DAY:

OTHER TO-DOS & BRAIN DUMP (NOTES):

6.00-6.30	
6.30-7.00	
7.00-7.30	
7.30-8.00	
8.00-8.30	
8.30-9.00	
9.00-9.30	
9.30-10.00	
10.00-10.30	
10.30-11.00	
11.00-11.30	
11.30-12.00	
12.00-12.30	
12.30-13.00	
13.00-13.30	
13.30-14.00	
14.00-14.30	
14.30-15.00	
15.00-15.30	
15.30-16.00	
16.00-16.30	
16.30-17.00	
17.30-18.00	
18.00-18.30	
18.30-19.00	
19.00-19.30	
19.30-20.00	
20.00-20.30	
20.30-21.00	

DATE: WEEK:

TODAY I FEEL (ON A SCALE FROM 1- 10): TO
INCREASE MY ENERGY I CAN:

WILD DAYDREAMS:

TODAYS MAIN OBJECTIVE AND FOCUS:

FROG OF THE DAY:

OTHER TO-DOS & BRAIN DUMP (NOTES):

6.00-6.30	
6.30-7.00	
7.00-7.30	
7.30-8.00	
8.00-8.30	
8.30-9.00	
9.00-9.30	
9.30-10.00	
10.00-10.30	
10.30-11.00	
11.00-11.30	
11.30-12.00	
12.00-12.30	
12.30-13.00	
13.00-13.30	
13.30-14.00	
14.00-14.30	
14.30-15.00	
15.00-15.30	
15.30-16.00	
16.00-16.30	
16.30-17.00	
17.30-18.00	
18.00-18.30	
18.30-19.00	
19.00-19.30	
19.30-20.00	
20.00-20.30	
20.30-21.00	

DATE: WEEK:

TODAY I FEEL (ON A SCALE FROM 1- 10): TO
INCREASE MY ENERGY I CAN:

WILD DAYDREAMS:

TODAYS MAIN OBJECTIVE AND FOCUS:

FROG OF THE DAY:

OTHER TO-DOS & BRAIN DUMP (NOTES):

6.00-6.30	
6.30-7.00	
7.00-7.30	
7.30-8.00	
8.00-8.30	
8.30-9.00	
9.00-9.30	
9.30-10.00	
10.00-10.30	
10.30-11.00	
11.00-11.30	
11.30-12.00	
12.00-12.30	
12.30-13.00	
13.00-13.30	
13.30-14.00	
14.00-14.30	
14.30-15.00	
15.00-15.30	
15.30-16.00	
16.00-16.30	
16.30-17.00	
17.30-18.00	
18.00-18.30	
18.30-19.00	
19.00-19.30	
19.30-20.00	
20.00-20.30	
20.30-21.00	

DATE: WEEK:

TODAY I FEEL (ON A SCALE FROM 1- 10): TO
INCREASE MY ENERGY I CAN:

WILD DAYDREAMS:

TODAYS MAIN OBJECTIVE AND FOCUS:

FROG OF THE DAY:

OTHER TO-DOS & BRAIN DUMP (NOTES):

6.00-6.30	
6.30-7.00	
7.00-7.30	
7.30-8.00	
8.00-8.30	
8.30-9.00	
9.00-9.30	
9.30-10.00	
10.00-10.30	
10.30-11.00	
11.00-11.30	
11.30-12.00	
12.00-12.30	
12.30-13.00	
13.00-13.30	
13.30-14.00	
14.00-14.30	
14.30-15.00	
15.00-15.30	
15.30-16.00	
16.00-16.30	
16.30-17.00	
17.30-18.00	
18.00-18.30	
18.30-19.00	
19.00-19.30	
19.30-20.00	
20.00-20.30	
20.30-21.00	

DATE: WEEK:

TODAY I FEEL (ON A SCALE FROM 1- 10): TO
INCREASE MY ENERGY I CAN:

WILD DAYDREAMS:

TODAYS MAIN OBJECTIVE AND FOCUS:

FROG OF THE DAY:

OTHER TO-DOS & BRAIN DUMP (NOTES):

6.00-6.30	
6.30-7.00	
7.00-7.30	
7.30-8.00	
8.00-8.30	
8.30-9.00	
9.00-9.30	
9.30-10.00	
10.00-10.30	
10.30-11.00	
11.00-11.30	
11.30-12.00	
12.00-12.30	
12.30-13.00	
13.00-13.30	
13.30-14.00	
14.00-14.30	
14.30-15.00	
15.00-15.30	
15.30-16.00	
16.00-16.30	
16.30-17.00	
17.30-18.00	
18.00-18.30	
18.30-19.00	
19.00-19.30	
19.30-20.00	
20.00-20.30	
20.30-21.00	

DATE: WEEK:

TODAY I FEEL (ON A SCALE FROM 1- 10): TO
INCREASE MY ENERGY I CAN:

WILD DAYDREAMS:

TODAYS MAIN OBJECTIVE AND FOCUS:

FROG OF THE DAY:

OTHER TO-DOS & BRAIN DUMP (NOTES):

6.00-6.30	
6.30-7.00	
7.00-7.30	
7.30-8.00	
8.00-8.30	
8.30-9.00	
9.00-9.30	
9.30-10.00	
10.00-10.30	
10.30-11.00	
11.00-11.30	
11.30-12.00	
12.00-12.30	
12.30-13.00	
13.00-13.30	
13.30-14.00	
14.00-14.30	
14.30-15.00	
15.00-15.30	
15.30-16.00	
16.00-16.30	
16.30-17.00	
17.30-18.00	
18.00-18.30	
18.30-19.00	
19.00-19.30	
19.30-20.00	
20.00-20.30	
20.30-21.00	

DATE: WEEK:

TODAY I FEEL (ON A SCALE FROM 1- 10): TO
INCREASE MY ENERGY I CAN:

WILD DAYDREAMS:

TODAYS MAIN OBJECTIVE AND FOCUS:

FROG OF THE DAY:

OTHER TO-DOS & BRAIN DUMP (NOTES):

Time	
6.00-6.30	
6.30-7.00	
7.00-7.30	
7.30-8.00	
8.00-8.30	
8.30-9.00	
9.00-9.30	
9.30-10.00	
10.00-10.30	
10.30-11.00	
11.00-11.30	
11.30-12.00	
12.00-12.30	
12.30-13.00	
13.00-13.30	
13.30-14.00	
14.00-14.30	
14.30-15.00	
15.00-15.30	
15.30-16.00	
16.00-16.30	
16.30-17.00	
17.30-18.00	
18.00-18.30	
18.30-19.00	
19.00-19.30	
19.30-20.00	
20.00-20.30	
20.30-21.00	

DATE: WEEK:

TODAY I FEEL (ON A SCALE FROM 1- 10): TO
INCREASE MY ENERGY I CAN:

WILD DAYDREAMS:

TODAYS MAIN OBJECTIVE AND FOCUS:

FROG OF THE DAY:

OTHER TO-DOS & BRAIN DUMP (NOTES):

6.00-6.30	
6.30-7.00	
7.00-7.30	
7.30-8.00	
8.00-8.30	
8.30-9.00	
9.00-9.30	
9.30-10.00	
10.00-10.30	
10.30-11.00	
11.00-11.30	
11.30-12.00	
12.00-12.30	
12.30-13.00	
13.00-13.30	
13.30-14.00	
14.00-14.30	
14.30-15.00	
15.00-15.30	
15.30-16.00	
16.00-16.30	
16.30-17.00	
17.30-18.00	
18.00-18.30	
18.30-19.00	
19.00-19.30	
19.30-20.00	
20.00-20.30	
20.30-21.00	

DATE: WEEK:

TODAY I FEEL (ON A SCALE FROM 1- 10): TO
INCREASE MY ENERGY I CAN:

WILD DAYDREAMS:

TODAYS MAIN OBJECTIVE AND FOCUS:

FROG OF THE DAY:

OTHER TO-DOS & BRAIN DUMP (NOTES):

6.00-6.30	
6.30-7.00	
7.00-7.30	
7.30-8.00	
8.00-8.30	
8.30-9.00	
9.00-9.30	
9.30-10.00	
10.00-10.30	
10.30-11.00	
11.00-11.30	
11.30-12.00	
12.00-12.30	
12.30-13.00	
13.00-13.30	
13.30-14.00	
14.00-14.30	
14.30-15.00	
15.00-15.30	
15.30-16.00	
16.00-16.30	
16.30-17.00	
17.30-18.00	
18.00-18.30	
18.30-19.00	
19.00-19.30	
19.30-20.00	
20.00-20.30	
20.30-21.00	

DATE: WEEK:

TODAY I FEEL (ON A SCALE FROM 1- 10): TO
INCREASE MY ENERGY I CAN:

WILD DAYDREAMS:

TODAYS MAIN OBJECTIVE AND FOCUS:

FROG OF THE DAY:

OTHER TO-DOS & BRAIN DUMP (NOTES):

Time	
6.00-6.30	
6.30-7.00	
7.00-7.30	
7.30-8.00	
8.00-8.30	
8.30-9.00	
9.00-9.30	
9.30-10.00	
10.00-10.30	
10.30-11.00	
11.00-11.30	
11.30-12.00	
12.00-12.30	
12.30-13.00	
13.00-13.30	
13.30-14.00	
14.00-14.30	
14.30-15.00	
15.00-15.30	
15.30-16.00	
16.00-16.30	
16.30-17.00	
17.30-18.00	
18.00-18.30	
18.30-19.00	
19.00-19.30	
19.30-20.00	
20.00-20.30	
20.30-21.00	

DATE: WEEK:

TODAY I FEEL (ON A SCALE FROM 1- 10): TO
INCREASE MY ENERGY I CAN:

WILD DAYDREAMS:

TODAYS MAIN OBJECTIVE AND FOCUS:

FROG OF THE DAY:

OTHER TO-DOS & BRAIN DUMP (NOTES):

6.00-6.30	
6.30-7.00	
7.00-7.30	
7.30-8.00	
8.00-8.30	
8.30-9.00	
9.00-9.30	
9.30-10.00	
10.00-10.30	
10.30-11.00	
11.00-11.30	
11.30-12.00	
12.00-12.30	
12.30-13.00	
13.00-13.30	
13.30-14.00	
14.00-14.30	
14.30-15.00	
15.00-15.30	
15.30-16.00	
16.00-16.30	
16.30-17.00	
17.30-18.00	
18.00-18.30	
18.30-19.00	
19.00-19.30	
19.30-20.00	
20.00-20.30	
20.30-21.00	

DATE: WEEK:

TODAY I FEEL (ON A SCALE FROM 1- 10): TO
INCREASE MY ENERGY I CAN:

WILD DAYDREAMS:

TODAYS MAIN OBJECTIVE AND FOCUS:

FROG OF THE DAY:

OTHER TO-DOS & BRAIN DUMP (NOTES):

6.00-6.30	
6.30-7.00	
7.00-7.30	
7.30-8.00	
8.00-8.30	
8.30-9.00	
9.00-9.30	
9.30-10.00	
10.00-10.30	
10.30-11.00	
11.00-11.30	
11.30-12.00	
12.00-12.30	
12.30-13.00	
13.00-13.30	
13.30-14.00	
14.00-14.30	
14.30-15.00	
15.00-15.30	
15.30-16.00	
16.00-16.30	
16.30-17.00	
17.30-18.00	
18.00-18.30	
18.30-19.00	
19.00-19.30	
19.30-20.00	
20.00-20.30	
20.30-21.00	

DATE: WEEK:

TODAY I FEEL (ON A SCALE FROM 1- 10): TO
INCREASE MY ENERGY I CAN:

WILD DAYDREAMS:

TODAYS MAIN OBJECTIVE AND FOCUS:

FROG OF THE DAY:

OTHER TO-DOS & BRAIN DUMP (NOTES):

6.00-6.30	
6.30-7.00	
7.00-7.30	
7.30-8.00	
8.00-8.30	
8.30-9.00	
9.00-9.30	
9.30-10.00	
10.00-10.30	
10.30-11.00	
11.00-11.30	
11.30-12.00	
12.00-12.30	
12.30-13.00	
13.00-13.30	
13.30-14.00	
14.00-14.30	
14.30-15.00	
15.00-15.30	
15.30-16.00	
16.00-16.30	
16.30-17.00	
17.30-18.00	
18.00-18.30	
18.30-19.00	
19.00-19.30	
19.30-20.00	
20.00-20.30	
20.30-21.00	

DATE: WEEK:

TODAY I FEEL (ON A SCALE FROM 1- 10): TO
INCREASE MY ENERGY I CAN:

WILD DAYDREAMS:

TODAYS MAIN OBJECTIVE AND FOCUS:

FROG OF THE DAY:

OTHER TO-DOS & BRAIN DUMP (NOTES):

6.00-6.30	
6.30-7.00	
7.00-7.30	
7.30-8.00	
8.00-8.30	
8.30-9.00	
9.00-9.30	
9.30-10.00	
10.00-10.30	
10.30-11.00	
11.00-11.30	
11.30-12.00	
12.00-12.30	
12.30-13.00	
13.00-13.30	
13.30-14.00	
14.00-14.30	
14.30-15.00	
15.00-15.30	
15.30-16.00	
16.00-16.30	
16.30-17.00	
17.30-18.00	
18.00-18.30	
18.30-19.00	
19.00-19.30	
19.30-20.00	
20.00-20.30	
20.30-21.00	

DATE: WEEK:

TODAY I FEEL (ON A SCALE FROM 1- 10): TO
INCREASE MY ENERGY I CAN:

WILD DAYDREAMS:

TODAYS MAIN OBJECTIVE AND FOCUS:

FROG OF THE DAY:

OTHER TO-DOS & BRAIN DUMP (NOTES):

6.00-6.30	
6.30-7.00	
7.00-7.30	
7.30-8.00	
8.00-8.30	
8.30-9.00	
9.00-9.30	
9.30-10.00	
10.00-10.30	
10.30-11.00	
11.00-11.30	
11.30-12.00	
12.00-12.30	
12.30-13.00	
13.00-13.30	
13.30-14.00	
14.00-14.30	
14.30-15.00	
15.00-15.30	
15.30-16.00	
16.00-16.30	
16.30-17.00	
17.30-18.00	
18.00-18.30	
18.30-19.00	
19.00-19.30	
19.30-20.00	
20.00-20.30	
20.30-21.00	

DATE: WEEK:

TODAY I FEEL (ON A SCALE FROM 1- 10): TO
INCREASE MY ENERGY I CAN:

WILD DAYDREAMS:

TODAYS MAIN OBJECTIVE AND FOCUS:

FROG OF THE DAY:

OTHER TO-DOS & BRAIN DUMP (NOTES):

6.00-6.30	
6.30-7.00	
7.00-7.30	
7.30-8.00	
8.00-8.30	
8.30-9.00	
9.00-9.30	
9.30-10.00	
10.00-10.30	
10.30-11.00	
11.00-11.30	
11.30-12.00	
12.00-12.30	
12.30-13.00	
13.00-13.30	
13.30-14.00	
14.00-14.30	
14.30-15.00	
15.00-15.30	
15.30-16.00	
16.00-16.30	
16.30-17.00	
17.30-18.00	
18.00-18.30	
18.30-19.00	
19.00-19.30	
19.30-20.00	
20.00-20.30	
20.30-21.00	

DATE: WEEK:

TODAY I FEEL (ON A SCALE FROM 1- 10): TO
INCREASE MY ENERGY I CAN:

WILD DAYDREAMS:

TODAYS MAIN OBJECTIVE AND FOCUS:

FROG OF THE DAY:

OTHER TO-DOS & BRAIN DUMP (NOTES):

6.00-6.30	
6.30-7.00	
7.00-7.30	
7.30-8.00	
8.00-8.30	
8.30-9.00	
9.00-9.30	
9.30-10.00	
10.00-10.30	
10.30-11.00	
11.00-11.30	
11.30-12.00	
12.00-12.30	
12.30-13.00	
13.00-13.30	
13.30-14.00	
14.00-14.30	
14.30-15.00	
15.00-15.30	
15.30-16.00	
16.00-16.30	
16.30-17.00	
17.30-18.00	
18.00-18.30	
18.30-19.00	
19.00-19.30	
19.30-20.00	
20.00-20.30	
20.30-21.00	

DATE: WEEK:

TODAY I FEEL (ON A SCALE FROM 1- 10): TO
INCREASE MY ENERGY I CAN:

WILD DAYDREAMS:

TODAYS MAIN OBJECTIVE AND FOCUS:

FROG OF THE DAY:

OTHER TO-DOS & BRAIN DUMP (NOTES):

6.00-6.30	
6.30-7.00	
7.00-7.30	
7.30-8.00	
8.00-8.30	
8.30-9.00	
9.00-9.30	
9.30-10.00	
10.00-10.30	
10.30-11.00	
11.00-11.30	
11.30-12.00	
12.00-12.30	
12.30-13.00	
13.00-13.30	
13.30-14.00	
14.00-14.30	
14.30-15.00	
15.00-15.30	
15.30-16.00	
16.00-16.30	
16.30-17.00	
17.30-18.00	
18.00-18.30	
18.30-19.00	
19.00-19.30	
19.30-20.00	
20.00-20.30	
20.30-21.00	

DATE: WEEK:

TODAY I FEEL (ON A SCALE FROM 1- 10): TO
INCREASE MY ENERGY I CAN:

WILD DAYDREAMS:

TODAYS MAIN OBJECTIVE AND FOCUS:

FROG OF THE DAY:

OTHER TO-DOS & BRAIN DUMP (NOTES):

6.00-6.30	
6.30-7.00	
7.00-7.30	
7.30-8.00	
8.00-8.30	
8.30-9.00	
9.00-9.30	
9.30-10.00	
10.00-10.30	
10.30-11.00	
11.00-11.30	
11.30-12.00	
12.00-12.30	
12.30-13.00	
13.00-13.30	
13.30-14.00	
14.00-14.30	
14.30-15.00	
15.00-15.30	
15.30-16.00	
16.00-16.30	
16.30-17.00	
17.30-18.00	
18.00-18.30	
18.30-19.00	
19.00-19.30	
19.30-20.00	
20.00-20.30	
20.30-21.00	

DATE: WEEK:

TODAY I FEEL (ON A SCALE FROM 1- 10): TO
INCREASE MY ENERGY I CAN:

WILD DAYDREAMS:

TODAYS MAIN OBJECTIVE AND FOCUS:

FROG OF THE DAY:

OTHER TO-DOS & BRAIN DUMP (NOTES):

6.00-6.30	
6.30-7.00	
7.00-7.30	
7.30-8.00	
8.00-8.30	
8.30-9.00	
9.00-9.30	
9.30-10.00	
10.00-10.30	
10.30-11.00	
11.00-11.30	
11.30-12.00	
12.00-12.30	
12.30-13.00	
13.00-13.30	
13.30-14.00	
14.00-14.30	
14.30-15.00	
15.00-15.30	
15.30-16.00	
16.00-16.30	
16.30-17.00	
17.30-18.00	
18.00-18.30	
18.30-19.00	
19.00-19.30	
19.30-20.00	
20.00-20.30	
20.30-21.00	

DATE: WEEK:

TODAY I FEEL (ON A SCALE FROM 1- 10): TO
INCREASE MY ENERGY I CAN:

WILD DAYDREAMS:

TODAYS MAIN OBJECTIVE AND FOCUS:

FROG OF THE DAY:

OTHER TO-DOS & BRAIN DUMP (NOTES):

6.00-6.30	
6.30-7.00	
7.00-7.30	
7.30-8.00	
8.00-8.30	
8.30-9.00	
9.00-9.30	
9.30-10.00	
10.00-10.30	
10.30-11.00	
11.00-11.30	
11.30-12.00	
12.00-12.30	
12.30-13.00	
13.00-13.30	
13.30-14.00	
14.00-14.30	
14.30-15.00	
15.00-15.30	
15.30-16.00	
16.00-16.30	
16.30-17.00	
17.30-18.00	
18.00-18.30	
18.30-19.00	
19.00-19.30	
19.30-20.00	
20.00-20.30	
20.30-21.00	

DATE: WEEK:

TODAY I FEEL (ON A SCALE FROM 1- 10): TO
INCREASE MY ENERGY I CAN:

WILD DAYDREAMS:

TODAYS MAIN OBJECTIVE AND FOCUS:

FROG OF THE DAY:

OTHER TO-DOS & BRAIN DUMP (NOTES):

6.00-6.30	
6.30-7.00	
7.00-7.30	
7.30-8.00	
8.00-8.30	
8.30-9.00	
9.00-9.30	
9.30-10.00	
10.00-10.30	
10.30-11.00	
11.00-11.30	
11.30-12.00	
12.00-12.30	
12.30-13.00	
13.00-13.30	
13.30-14.00	
14.00-14.30	
14.30-15.00	
15.00-15.30	
15.30-16.00	
16.00-16.30	
16.30-17.00	
17.30-18.00	
18.00-18.30	
18.30-19.00	
19.00-19.30	
19.30-20.00	
20.00-20.30	
20.30-21.00	

DATE: WEEK:

TODAY I FEEL (ON A SCALE FROM 1- 10): TO
INCREASE MY ENERGY I CAN:

WILD DAYDREAMS:

TODAYS MAIN OBJECTIVE AND FOCUS:

FROG OF THE DAY:

OTHER TO-DOS & BRAIN DUMP (NOTES):

6.00-6.30	
6.30-7.00	
7.00-7.30	
7.30-8.00	
8.00-8.30	
8.30-9.00	
9.00-9.30	
9.30-10.00	
10.00-10.30	
10.30-11.00	
11.00-11.30	
11.30-12.00	
12.00-12.30	
12.30-13.00	
13.00-13.30	
13.30-14.00	
14.00-14.30	
14.30-15.00	
15.00-15.30	
15.30-16.00	
16.00-16.30	
16.30-17.00	
17.30-18.00	
18.00-18.30	
18.30-19.00	
19.00-19.30	
19.30-20.00	
20.00-20.30	
20.30-21.00	

DATE: WEEK:

TODAY I FEEL (ON A SCALE FROM 1- 10): TO
INCREASE MY ENERGY I CAN:

WILD DAYDREAMS:

TODAYS MAIN OBJECTIVE AND FOCUS:

FROG OF THE DAY:

OTHER TO-DOS & BRAIN DUMP (NOTES):

6.00-6.30	
6.30-7.00	
7.00-7.30	
7.30-8.00	
8.00-8.30	
8.30-9.00	
9.00-9.30	
9.30-10.00	
10.00-10.30	
10.30-11.00	
11.00-11.30	
11.30-12.00	
12.00-12.30	
12.30-13.00	
13.00-13.30	
13.30-14.00	
14.00-14.30	
14.30-15.00	
15.00-15.30	
15.30-16.00	
16.00-16.30	
16.30-17.00	
17.30-18.00	
18.00-18.30	
18.30-19.00	
19.00-19.30	
19.30-20.00	
20.00-20.30	
20.30-21.00	

DATE: WEEK:

TODAY I FEEL (ON A SCALE FROM 1- 10): TO
INCREASE MY ENERGY I CAN:

WILD DAYDREAMS:

TODAYS MAIN OBJECTIVE AND FOCUS:

FROG OF THE DAY:

OTHER TO-DOS & BRAIN DUMP (NOTES):

6.00-6.30	
6.30-7.00	
7.00-7.30	
7.30-8.00	
8.00-8.30	
8.30-9.00	
9.00-9.30	
9.30-10.00	
10.00-10.30	
10.30-11.00	
11.00-11.30	
11.30-12.00	
12.00-12.30	
12.30-13.00	
13.00-13.30	
13.30-14.00	
14.00-14.30	
14.30-15.00	
15.00-15.30	
15.30-16.00	
16.00-16.30	
16.30-17.00	
17.30-18.00	
18.00-18.30	
18.30-19.00	
19.00-19.30	
19.30-20.00	
20.00-20.30	
20.30-21.00	

DATE: WEEK:

TODAY I FEEL (ON A SCALE FROM 1- 10): TO
INCREASE MY ENERGY I CAN:

WILD DAYDREAMS:

TODAYS MAIN OBJECTIVE AND FOCUS:

FROG OF THE DAY:

OTHER TO-DOS & BRAIN DUMP (NOTES):

6.00-6.30	
6.30-7.00	
7.00-7.30	
7.30-8.00	
8.00-8.30	
8.30-9.00	
9.00-9.30	
9.30-10.00	
10.00-10.30	
10.30-11.00	
11.00-11.30	
11.30-12.00	
12.00-12.30	
12.30-13.00	
13.00-13.30	
13.30-14.00	
14.00-14.30	
14.30-15.00	
15.00-15.30	
15.30-16.00	
16.00-16.30	
16.30-17.00	
17.30-18.00	
18.00-18.30	
18.30-19.00	
19.00-19.30	
19.30-20.00	
20.00-20.30	
20.30-21.00	

DATE: WEEK:

TODAY I FEEL (ON A SCALE FROM 1- 10): TO
INCREASE MY ENERGY I CAN:

WILD DAYDREAMS:

TODAYS MAIN OBJECTIVE AND FOCUS:

FROG OF THE DAY:

OTHER TO-DOS & BRAIN DUMP (NOTES):

6.00-6.30	
6.30-7.00	
7.00-7.30	
7.30-8.00	
8.00-8.30	
8.30-9.00	
9.00-9.30	
9.30-10.00	
10.00-10.30	
10.30-11.00	
11.00-11.30	
11.30-12.00	
12.00-12.30	
12.30-13.00	
13.00-13.30	
13.30-14.00	
14.00-14.30	
14.30-15.00	
15.00-15.30	
15.30-16.00	
16.00-16.30	
16.30-17.00	
17.30-18.00	
18.00-18.30	
18.30-19.00	
19.00-19.30	
19.30-20.00	
20.00-20.30	
20.30-21.00	

DATE: WEEK:

TODAY I FEEL (ON A SCALE FROM 1- 10): TO
INCREASE MY ENERGY I CAN:

WILD DAYDREAMS:

TODAYS MAIN OBJECTIVE AND FOCUS:

FROG OF THE DAY:

OTHER TO-DOS & BRAIN DUMP (NOTES):

Time	
6.00-6.30	
6.30-7.00	
7.00-7.30	
7.30-8.00	
8.00-8.30	
8.30-9.00	
9.00-9.30	
9.30-10.00	
10.00-10.30	
10.30-11.00	
11.00-11.30	
11.30-12.00	
12.00-12.30	
12.30-13.00	
13.00-13.30	
13.30-14.00	
14.00-14.30	
14.30-15.00	
15.00-15.30	
15.30-16.00	
16.00-16.30	
16.30-17.00	
17.30-18.00	
18.00-18.30	
18.30-19.00	
19.00-19.30	
19.30-20.00	
20.00-20.30	
20.30-21.00	

DATE: WEEK:

TODAY I FEEL (ON A SCALE FROM 1- 10): TO
INCREASE MY ENERGY I CAN:

WILD DAYDREAMS:

TODAYS MAIN OBJECTIVE AND FOCUS:

FROG OF THE DAY:

OTHER TO-DOS & BRAIN DUMP (NOTES):

6.00-6.30	
6.30-7.00	
7.00-7.30	
7.30-8.00	
8.00-8.30	
8.30-9.00	
9.00-9.30	
9.30-10.00	
10.00-10.30	
10.30-11.00	
11.00-11.30	
11.30-12.00	
12.00-12.30	
12.30-13.00	
13.00-13.30	
13.30-14.00	
14.00-14.30	
14.30-15.00	
15.00-15.30	
15.30-16.00	
16.00-16.30	
16.30-17.00	
17.30-18.00	
18.00-18.30	
18.30-19.00	
19.00-19.30	
19.30-20.00	
20.00-20.30	
20.30-21.00	

DATE: WEEK:

TODAY I FEEL (ON A SCALE FROM 1- 10): TO
INCREASE MY ENERGY I CAN:

WILD DAYDREAMS:

TODAYS MAIN OBJECTIVE AND FOCUS:

FROG OF THE DAY:

OTHER TO-DOS & BRAIN DUMP (NOTES):

6.00-6.30	
6.30-7.00	
7.00-7.30	
7.30-8.00	
8.00-8.30	
8.30-9.00	
9.00-9.30	
9.30-10.00	
10.00-10.30	
10.30-11.00	
11.00-11.30	
11.30-12.00	
12.00-12.30	
12.30-13.00	
13.00-13.30	
13.30-14.00	
14.00-14.30	
14.30-15.00	
15.00-15.30	
15.30-16.00	
16.00-16.30	
16.30-17.00	
17.30-18.00	
18.00-18.30	
18.30-19.00	
19.00-19.30	
19.30-20.00	
20.00-20.30	
20.30-21.00	

DATE: WEEK:

TODAY I FEEL (ON A SCALE FROM 1- 10): TO
INCREASE MY ENERGY I CAN:

WILD DAYDREAMS:

TODAYS MAIN OBJECTIVE AND FOCUS:

FROG OF THE DAY:

OTHER TO-DOS & BRAIN DUMP (NOTES):

6.00-6.30	
6.30-7.00	
7.00-7.30	
7.30-8.00	
8.00-8.30	
8.30-9.00	
9.00-9.30	
9.30-10.00	
10.00-10.30	
10.30-11.00	
11.00-11.30	
11.30-12.00	
12.00-12.30	
12.30-13.00	
13.00-13.30	
13.30-14.00	
14.00-14.30	
14.30-15.00	
15.00-15.30	
15.30-16.00	
16.00-16.30	
16.30-17.00	
17.30-18.00	
18.00-18.30	
18.30-19.00	
19.00-19.30	
19.30-20.00	
20.00-20.30	
20.30-21.00	

DATE: WEEK:

TODAY I FEEL (ON A SCALE FROM 1- 10): TO
INCREASE MY ENERGY I CAN:

WILD DAYDREAMS:

TODAYS MAIN OBJECTIVE AND FOCUS:

FROG OF THE DAY:

OTHER TO-DOS & BRAIN DUMP (NOTES):

6.00-6.30	
6.30-7.00	
7.00-7.30	
7.30-8.00	
8.00-8.30	
8.30-9.00	
9.00-9.30	
9.30-10.00	
10.00-10.30	
10.30-11.00	
11.00-11.30	
11.30-12.00	
12.00-12.30	
12.30-13.00	
13.00-13.30	
13.30-14.00	
14.00-14.30	
14.30-15.00	
15.00-15.30	
15.30-16.00	
16.00-16.30	
16.30-17.00	
17.30-18.00	
18.00-18.30	
18.30-19.00	
19.00-19.30	
19.30-20.00	
20.00-20.30	
20.30-21.00	

DATE: WEEK:

TODAY I FEEL (ON A SCALE FROM 1- 10): TO
INCREASE MY ENERGY I CAN:

WILD DAYDREAMS:

TODAYS MAIN OBJECTIVE AND FOCUS:

FROG OF THE DAY:

OTHER TO-DOS & BRAIN DUMP (NOTES):

6.00-6.30	
6.30-7.00	
7.00-7.30	
7.30-8.00	
8.00-8.30	
8.30-9.00	
9.00-9.30	
9.30-10.00	
10.00-10.30	
10.30-11.00	
11.00-11.30	
11.30-12.00	
12.00-12.30	
12.30-13.00	
13.00-13.30	
13.30-14.00	
14.00-14.30	
14.30-15.00	
15.00-15.30	
15.30-16.00	
16.00-16.30	
16.30-17.00	
17.30-18.00	
18.00-18.30	
18.30-19.00	
19.00-19.30	
19.30-20.00	
20.00-20.30	
20.30-21.00	

DATE: WEEK:

TODAY I FEEL (ON A SCALE FROM 1- 10): TO
INCREASE MY ENERGY I CAN:

WILD DAYDREAMS:

TODAYS MAIN OBJECTIVE AND FOCUS:

FROG OF THE DAY:

OTHER TO-DOS & BRAIN DUMP (NOTES):

6.00-6.30	
6.30-7.00	
7.00-7.30	
7.30-8.00	
8.00-8.30	
8.30-9.00	
9.00-9.30	
9.30-10.00	
10.00-10.30	
10.30-11.00	
11.00-11.30	
11.30-12.00	
12.00-12.30	
12.30-13.00	
13.00-13.30	
13.30-14.00	
14.00-14.30	
14.30-15.00	
15.00-15.30	
15.30-16.00	
16.00-16.30	
16.30-17.00	
17.30-18.00	
18.00-18.30	
18.30-19.00	
19.00-19.30	
19.30-20.00	
20.00-20.30	
20.30-21.00	

DATE: WEEK:

TODAY I FEEL (ON A SCALE FROM 1- 10): TO
INCREASE MY ENERGY I CAN:

WILD DAYDREAMS:

TODAYS MAIN OBJECTIVE AND FOCUS:

FROG OF THE DAY:

OTHER TO-DOS & BRAIN DUMP (NOTES):

6.00-6.30	
6.30-7.00	
7.00-7.30	
7.30-8.00	
8.00-8.30	
8.30-9.00	
9.00-9.30	
9.30-10.00	
10.00-10.30	
10.30-11.00	
11.00-11.30	
11.30-12.00	
12.00-12.30	
12.30-13.00	
13.00-13.30	
13.30-14.00	
14.00-14.30	
14.30-15.00	
15.00-15.30	
15.30-16.00	
16.00-16.30	
16.30-17.00	
17.30-18.00	
18.00-18.30	
18.30-19.00	
19.00-19.30	
19.30-20.00	
20.00-20.30	
20.30-21.00	

DATE: WEEK:

TODAY I FEEL (ON A SCALE FROM 1- 10): TO
INCREASE MY ENERGY I CAN:

WILD DAYDREAMS:

TODAYS MAIN OBJECTIVE AND FOCUS:

FROG OF THE DAY:

OTHER TO-DOS & BRAIN DUMP (NOTES):

6.00-6.30	
6.30-7.00	
7.00-7.30	
7.30-8.00	
8.00-8.30	
8.30-9.00	
9.00-9.30	
9.30-10.00	
10.00-10.30	
10.30-11.00	
11.00-11.30	
11.30-12.00	
12.00-12.30	
12.30-13.00	
13.00-13.30	
13.30-14.00	
14.00-14.30	
14.30-15.00	
15.00-15.30	
15.30-16.00	
16.00-16.30	
16.30-17.00	
17.30-18.00	
18.00-18.30	
18.30-19.00	
19.00-19.30	
19.30-20.00	
20.00-20.30	
20.30-21.00	

DATE: WEEK:

TODAY I FEEL (ON A SCALE FROM 1- 10): TO
INCREASE MY ENERGY I CAN:

WILD DAYDREAMS:

TODAYS MAIN OBJECTIVE AND FOCUS:

FROG OF THE DAY:

OTHER TO-DOS & BRAIN DUMP (NOTES):

Time	
6.00-6.30	
6.30-7.00	
7.00-7.30	
7.30-8.00	
8.00-8.30	
8.30-9.00	
9.00-9.30	
9.30-10.00	
10.00-10.30	
10.30-11.00	
11.00-11.30	
11.30-12.00	
12.00-12.30	
12.30-13.00	
13.00-13.30	
13.30-14.00	
14.00-14.30	
14.30-15.00	
15.00-15.30	
15.30-16.00	
16.00-16.30	
16.30-17.00	
17.30-18.00	
18.00-18.30	
18.30-19.00	
19.00-19.30	
19.30-20.00	
20.00-20.30	
20.30-21.00	

DATE: WEEK:

TODAY I FEEL (ON A SCALE FROM 1- 10): TO
INCREASE MY ENERGY I CAN:

WILD DAYDREAMS:

TODAYS MAIN OBJECTIVE AND FOCUS:

FROG OF THE DAY:

OTHER TO-DOS & BRAIN DUMP (NOTES):

6.00-6.30	
6.30-7.00	
7.00-7.30	
7.30-8.00	
8.00-8.30	
8.30-9.00	
9.00-9.30	
9.30-10.00	
10.00-10.30	
10.30-11.00	
11.00-11.30	
11.30-12.00	
12.00-12.30	
12.30-13.00	
13.00-13.30	
13.30-14.00	
14.00-14.30	
14.30-15.00	
15.00-15.30	
15.30-16.00	
16.00-16.30	
16.30-17.00	
17.30-18.00	
18.00-18.30	
18.30-19.00	
19.00-19.30	
19.30-20.00	
20.00-20.30	
20.30-21.00	

DATE: WEEK:

TODAY I FEEL (ON A SCALE FROM 1- 10): TO
INCREASE MY ENERGY I CAN:

WILD DAYDREAMS:

TODAYS MAIN OBJECTIVE AND FOCUS:

FROG OF THE DAY:

OTHER TO-DOS & BRAIN DUMP (NOTES):

6.00-6.30	
6.30-7.00	
7.00-7.30	
7.30-8.00	
8.00-8.30	
8.30-9.00	
9.00-9.30	
9.30-10.00	
10.00-10.30	
10.30-11.00	
11.00-11.30	
11.30-12.00	
12.00-12.30	
12.30-13.00	
13.00-13.30	
13.30-14.00	
14.00-14.30	
14.30-15.00	
15.00-15.30	
15.30-16.00	
16.00-16.30	
16.30-17.00	
17.30-18.00	
18.00-18.30	
18.30-19.00	
19.00-19.30	
19.30-20.00	
20.00-20.30	
20.30-21.00	

DATE: WEEK:

TODAY I FEEL (ON A SCALE FROM 1- 10): TO
INCREASE MY ENERGY I CAN:

WILD DAYDREAMS:

TODAYS MAIN OBJECTIVE AND FOCUS:

FROG OF THE DAY:

OTHER TO-DOS & BRAIN DUMP (NOTES):

6.00-6.30	
6.30-7.00	
7.00-7.30	
7.30-8.00	
8.00-8.30	
8.30-9.00	
9.00-9.30	
9.30-10.00	
10.00-10.30	
10.30-11.00	
11.00-11.30	
11.30-12.00	
12.00-12.30	
12.30-13.00	
13.00-13.30	
13.30-14.00	
14.00-14.30	
14.30-15.00	
15.00-15.30	
15.30-16.00	
16.00-16.30	
16.30-17.00	
17.30-18.00	
18.00-18.30	
18.30-19.00	
19.00-19.30	
19.30-20.00	
20.00-20.30	
20.30-21.00	

DATE: WEEK:

TODAY I FEEL (ON A SCALE FROM 1- 10): TO
INCREASE MY ENERGY I CAN:

WILD DAYDREAMS:

TODAYS MAIN OBJECTIVE AND FOCUS:

FROG OF THE DAY:

OTHER TO-DOS & BRAIN DUMP (NOTES):

6.00-6.30	
6.30-7.00	
7.00-7.30	
7.30-8.00	
8.00-8.30	
8.30-9.00	
9.00-9.30	
9.30-10.00	
10.00-10.30	
10.30-11.00	
11.00-11.30	
11.30-12.00	
12.00-12.30	
12.30-13.00	
13.00-13.30	
13.30-14.00	
14.00-14.30	
14.30-15.00	
15.00-15.30	
15.30-16.00	
16.00-16.30	
16.30-17.00	
17.30-18.00	
18.00-18.30	
18.30-19.00	
19.00-19.30	
19.30-20.00	
20.00-20.30	
20.30-21.00	

DATE: WEEK:

TODAY I FEEL (ON A SCALE FROM 1- 10): TO
INCREASE MY ENERGY I CAN:

WILD DAYDREAMS:

TODAYS MAIN OBJECTIVE AND FOCUS:

FROG OF THE DAY:

OTHER TO-DOS & BRAIN DUMP (NOTES):

6.00-6.30	
6.30-7.00	
7.00-7.30	
7.30-8.00	
8.00-8.30	
8.30-9.00	
9.00-9.30	
9.30-10.00	
10.00-10.30	
10.30-11.00	
11.00-11.30	
11.30-12.00	
12.00-12.30	
12.30-13.00	
13.00-13.30	
13.30-14.00	
14.00-14.30	
14.30-15.00	
15.00-15.30	
15.30-16.00	
16.00-16.30	
16.30-17.00	
17.30-18.00	
18.00-18.30	
18.30-19.00	
19.00-19.30	
19.30-20.00	
20.00-20.30	
20.30-21.00	

DATE: WEEK:

TODAY I FEEL (ON A SCALE FROM 1- 10): TO
INCREASE MY ENERGY I CAN:

WILD DAYDREAMS:

TODAYS MAIN OBJECTIVE AND FOCUS:

FROG OF THE DAY:

OTHER TO-DOS & BRAIN DUMP (NOTES):

6.00-6.30	
6.30-7.00	
7.00-7.30	
7.30-8.00	
8.00-8.30	
8.30-9.00	
9.00-9.30	
9.30-10.00	
10.00-10.30	
10.30-11.00	
11.00-11.30	
11.30-12.00	
12.00-12.30	
12.30-13.00	
13.00-13.30	
13.30-14.00	
14.00-14.30	
14.30-15.00	
15.00-15.30	
15.30-16.00	
16.00-16.30	
16.30-17.00	
17.30-18.00	
18.00-18.30	
18.30-19.00	
19.00-19.30	
19.30-20.00	
20.00-20.30	
20.30-21.00	

DATE: WEEK:

TODAY I FEEL (ON A SCALE FROM 1- 10): TO
INCREASE MY ENERGY I CAN:

WILD DAYDREAMS:

TODAYS MAIN OBJECTIVE AND FOCUS:

FROG OF THE DAY:

OTHER TO-DOS & BRAIN DUMP (NOTES):

6.00-6.30	
6.30-7.00	
7.00-7.30	
7.30-8.00	
8.00-8.30	
8.30-9.00	
9.00-9.30	
9.30-10.00	
10.00-10.30	
10.30-11.00	
11.00-11.30	
11.30-12.00	
12.00-12.30	
12.30-13.00	
13.00-13.30	
13.30-14.00	
14.00-14.30	
14.30-15.00	
15.00-15.30	
15.30-16.00	
16.00-16.30	
16.30-17.00	
17.30-18.00	
18.00-18.30	
18.30-19.00	
19.00-19.30	
19.30-20.00	
20.00-20.30	
20.30-21.00	

DATE: WEEK:

TODAY I FEEL (ON A SCALE FROM 1- 10): TO
INCREASE MY ENERGY I CAN:

WILD DAYDREAMS:

TODAYS MAIN OBJECTIVE AND FOCUS:

FROG OF THE DAY:

OTHER TO-DOS & BRAIN DUMP (NOTES):

6.00-6.30	
6.30-7.00	
7.00-7.30	
7.30-8.00	
8.00-8.30	
8.30-9.00	
9.00-9.30	
9.30-10.00	
10.00-10.30	
10.30-11.00	
11.00-11.30	
11.30-12.00	
12.00-12.30	
12.30-13.00	
13.00-13.30	
13.30-14.00	
14.00-14.30	
14.30-15.00	
15.00-15.30	
15.30-16.00	
16.00-16.30	
16.30-17.00	
17.30-18.00	
18.00-18.30	
18.30-19.00	
19.00-19.30	
19.30-20.00	
20.00-20.30	
20.30-21.00	

DATE: WEEK:

TODAY I FEEL (ON A SCALE FROM 1- 10): TO
INCREASE MY ENERGY I CAN:

WILD DAYDREAMS:

TODAYS MAIN OBJECTIVE AND FOCUS:

FROG OF THE DAY:

OTHER TO-DOS & BRAIN DUMP (NOTES):

6.00-6.30	
6.30-7.00	
7.00-7.30	
7.30-8.00	
8.00-8.30	
8.30-9.00	
9.00-9.30	
9.30-10.00	
10.00-10.30	
10.30-11.00	
11.00-11.30	
11.30-12.00	
12.00-12.30	
12.30-13.00	
13.00-13.30	
13.30-14.00	
14.00-14.30	
14.30-15.00	
15.00-15.30	
15.30-16.00	
16.00-16.30	
16.30-17.00	
17.30-18.00	
18.00-18.30	
18.30-19.00	
19.00-19.30	
19.30-20.00	
20.00-20.30	
20.30-21.00	

DATE: WEEK:

TODAY I FEEL (ON A SCALE FROM 1- 10): TO
INCREASE MY ENERGY I CAN:

WILD DAYDREAMS:

TODAYS MAIN OBJECTIVE AND FOCUS:

FROG OF THE DAY:

OTHER TO-DOS & BRAIN DUMP (NOTES):

6.00-6.30	
6.30-7.00	
7.00-7.30	
7.30-8.00	
8.00-8.30	
8.30-9.00	
9.00-9.30	
9.30-10.00	
10.00-10.30	
10.30-11.00	
11.00-11.30	
11.30-12.00	
12.00-12.30	
12.30-13.00	
13.00-13.30	
13.30-14.00	
14.00-14.30	
14.30-15.00	
15.00-15.30	
15.30-16.00	
16.00-16.30	
16.30-17.00	
17.30-18.00	
18.00-18.30	
18.30-19.00	
19.00-19.30	
19.30-20.00	
20.00-20.30	
20.30-21.00	

DATE: WEEK:

TODAY I FEEL (ON A SCALE FROM 1- 10): TO
INCREASE MY ENERGY I CAN:

WILD DAYDREAMS:

TODAYS MAIN OBJECTIVE AND FOCUS:

FROG OF THE DAY:

OTHER TO-DOS & BRAIN DUMP (NOTES):

6.00-6.30	
6.30-7.00	
7.00-7.30	
7.30-8.00	
8.00-8.30	
8.30-9.00	
9.00-9.30	
9.30-10.00	
10.00-10.30	
10.30-11.00	
11.00-11.30	
11.30-12.00	
12.00-12.30	
12.30-13.00	
13.00-13.30	
13.30-14.00	
14.00-14.30	
14.30-15.00	
15.00-15.30	
15.30-16.00	
16.00-16.30	
16.30-17.00	
17.30-18.00	
18.00-18.30	
18.30-19.00	
19.00-19.30	
19.30-20.00	
20.00-20.30	
20.30-21.00	

DATE: WEEK:

TODAY I FEEL (ON A SCALE FROM 1- 10): TO
INCREASE MY ENERGY I CAN:

WILD DAYDREAMS:

TODAYS MAIN OBJECTIVE AND FOCUS:

FROG OF THE DAY:

OTHER TO-DOS & BRAIN DUMP (NOTES):

6.00-6.30	
6.30-7.00	
7.00-7.30	
7.30-8.00	
8.00-8.30	
8.30-9.00	
9.00-9.30	
9.30-10.00	
10.00-10.30	
10.30-11.00	
11.00-11.30	
11.30-12.00	
12.00-12.30	
12.30-13.00	
13.00-13.30	
13.30-14.00	
14.00-14.30	
14.30-15.00	
15.00-15.30	
15.30-16.00	
16.00-16.30	
16.30-17.00	
17.30-18.00	
18.00-18.30	
18.30-19.00	
19.00-19.30	
19.30-20.00	
20.00-20.30	
20.30-21.00	

DATE: WEEK:

TODAY I FEEL (ON A SCALE FROM 1- 10): TO
INCREASE MY ENERGY I CAN:

WILD DAYDREAMS:

TODAYS MAIN OBJECTIVE AND FOCUS:

FROG OF THE DAY:

OTHER TO-DOS & BRAIN DUMP (NOTES):

6.00-6.30	
6.30-7.00	
7.00-7.30	
7.30-8.00	
8.00-8.30	
8.30-9.00	
9.00-9.30	
9.30-10.00	
10.00-10.30	
10.30-11.00	
11.00-11.30	
11.30-12.00	
12.00-12.30	
12.30-13.00	
13.00-13.30	
13.30-14.00	
14.00-14.30	
14.30-15.00	
15.00-15.30	
15.30-16.00	
16.00-16.30	
16.30-17.00	
17.30-18.00	
18.00-18.30	
18.30-19.00	
19.00-19.30	
19.30-20.00	
20.00-20.30	
20.30-21.00	

DATE: WEEK:

TODAY I FEEL (ON A SCALE FROM 1- 10): TO
INCREASE MY ENERGY I CAN:

WILD DAYDREAMS:

TODAYS MAIN OBJECTIVE AND FOCUS:

FROG OF THE DAY:

OTHER TO-DOS & BRAIN DUMP (NOTES):

6.00-6.30	
6.30-7.00	
7.00-7.30	
7.30-8.00	
8.00-8.30	
8.30-9.00	
9.00-9.30	
9.30-10.00	
10.00-10.30	
10.30-11.00	
11.00-11.30	
11.30-12.00	
12.00-12.30	
12.30-13.00	
13.00-13.30	
13.30-14.00	
14.00-14.30	
14.30-15.00	
15.00-15.30	
15.30-16.00	
16.00-16.30	
16.30-17.00	
17.30-18.00	
18.00-18.30	
18.30-19.00	
19.00-19.30	
19.30-20.00	
20.00-20.30	
20.30-21.00	

DATE: WEEK:

TODAY I FEEL (ON A SCALE FROM 1- 10): TO
INCREASE MY ENERGY I CAN:

WILD DAYDREAMS:

TODAYS MAIN OBJECTIVE AND FOCUS:

FROG OF THE DAY:

OTHER TO-DOS & BRAIN DUMP (NOTES):

6.00-6.30	
6.30-7.00	
7.00-7.30	
7.30-8.00	
8.00-8.30	
8.30-9.00	
9.00-9.30	
9.30-10.00	
10.00-10.30	
10.30-11.00	
11.00-11.30	
11.30-12.00	
12.00-12.30	
12.30-13.00	
13.00-13.30	
13.30-14.00	
14.00-14.30	
14.30-15.00	
15.00-15.30	
15.30-16.00	
16.00-16.30	
16.30-17.00	
17.30-18.00	
18.00-18.30	
18.30-19.00	
19.00-19.30	
19.30-20.00	
20.00-20.30	
20.30-21.00	

DATE: WEEK:

TODAY I FEEL (ON A SCALE FROM 1- 10): TO
INCREASE MY ENERGY I CAN:

WILD DAYDREAMS:

TODAYS MAIN OBJECTIVE AND FOCUS:

FROG OF THE DAY:

OTHER TO-DOS & BRAIN DUMP (NOTES):

6.00-6.30	
6.30-7.00	
7.00-7.30	
7.30-8.00	
8.00-8.30	
8.30-9.00	
9.00-9.30	
9.30-10.00	
10.00-10.30	
10.30-11.00	
11.00-11.30	
11.30-12.00	
12.00-12.30	
12.30-13.00	
13.00-13.30	
13.30-14.00	
14.00-14.30	
14.30-15.00	
15.00-15.30	
15.30-16.00	
16.00-16.30	
16.30-17.00	
17.30-18.00	
18.00-18.30	
18.30-19.00	
19.00-19.30	
19.30-20.00	
20.00-20.30	
20.30-21.00	